Orthodox Churches

Geoff Robson

Heinemann
LIBRARY

First published in Great Britain by Heinemann Library
Halley Court, Jordan Hill, Oxford OX2 8EJ
a division of Reed Educational and Professional Publishing Ltd.
Heinemann is a registered trademark of Reed Educational & Professional Publishing Limited.

OXFORD MELBOURNE AUCKLAND
JOHANNESBURG IBADAN BLANTYRE GABORONE
PORTSMOUTH NH (USA) CHICAGO

Designed by Tinstar Design (www.tinstar.co.uk)
Illustrations by Martin Griffin and Nicholas Beresford-Davies
Printed by South China Printing in Hong Kong / China

03 02 01 00 99
10 9 8 7 6 5 4 3 2 1

British Library Cataloguing in Publication Data

Robson, Geoff
    Orthodox churches. - (Places of worship)
    1. Orthodox Eastern church buildings - Juvenile literature
    I. Title
    246.9'5819

ISBN 0 431 05184 4

Acknowledgements

The Publishers would like to thank the following for permission to reproduce photographs: Andes Press Agency/Carlos-Reyes Manzo, p.19; Birmingham City Council, pp.9, 10; Burrows, Adrian p.12; Circa Photo Library/Ged Murray, p.21; Impact Photos/Mohamed Ansar, p.20; Jackson, Rosemary, pp.15, 16, 17; Nesbitt, Eleanor, p.18; Roberts, Peter, p.5, St. Lazar's Dept. of Education, Bourneville, p.11; Woolridge, Jerry, pp.4, 6, 7, 8, 13, 14.

Cover photograph of the Church of the Holy Transfiguration, Coventry reproduced with permission of the author.

Our thanks to Philip Emmett for his comments in the preparation of this book, and to Louise Spilsbury for all her hard work.

The author would like to thank the following members of the Orthodox Church for their help: Mrs Nina Chapman, Father Daniel Joseph, Mrs Helen Maoudis, Mr Charis Mettis, Deacon John Nankivell, Deacon Stephen Platt, Father Milenko Zebic.

Every effort has been made to contact copyright holders of any material reproduced in this book. Any omissions will be rectified in subsequent printings if notice is given to the Publisher.

Contents

Words printed in **bold letters like these**
are explained in the Glossary.

Who uses Orthodox churches?

Orthodox Christians brought their religion to Britain and elsewhere when they left their own countries to escape wars or other problems. These Christians wanted to **worship** in the way they had always done.

At home they pray as a family in front of pictures, called **icons**. On Sundays and times like Easter, they also worship with other Orthodox Christians in special buildings called churches.

An Orthodox family prays at their icon corner.

This map shows some countries from which Orthodox Christians came to Britain.

Britain
Russia
Ukraine
Serbia
Greece
Cyprus

Where are they?

Orthodox churches are usually found in large towns and cities. Many are in buildings which once belonged to another Christian group. Some have been specially designed for Orthodox worship.

Some Orthodox churches have a **community centre** beside them. Here people born locally learn about their religion and the customs of the countries it came from.

This church in Coventry, England, was built for Greek Orthodox Christians.

What do they look like?

The outside of an **Orthodox** church may be very plain, with only a **cross** to tell you it is a church. It may also have a small belfry (bell tower) and a **dome** in the centre of the roof.

Most Orthodox churches are simple outside, so that the inside will look even more beautiful.

A Serbian Orthodox church in Birmingham, England.

Going inside

When Orthodox **worshippers** go into their church, they use gestures to show their devotion to **God**.

They make the **sign of the cross**, take a candle and walk respectfully up to a desk. On it is an **icon**. This **holy** picture shows the person or story that **Christians** remember at that time of year. The worshippers kiss the icon, then light their candles, placing them in a stand. The candle flame shines like their love for God.

Worshippers kiss the icon when they first enter the church.

What will I see first?

In **Orthodox** churches **icons** usually cover the walls and the ceiling. These icons are arranged to tell the story of **Jesus** and his **disciples**, linking them with other famous people from the **Bible**.

The most beautiful icons cover the **iconostasis**. This is a screen with doors in it. It divides the main part of the church from the **sanctuary**. In the sanctuary is a special table called the **altar**, and other things used in **worship**.

Looking towards the iconostasis.

Icons

Icons teach the Orthodox belief that **Jesus** is the Son of **God**. In the **dome** of many churches there is an icon of Jesus, shown as **Christ**, Lord of the Universe. Above the sanctuary there is usually an icon of Mary, his mother. Other icons are of the **saints**, people who once lived close to God and are now believed to be worshipping God in **heaven**.

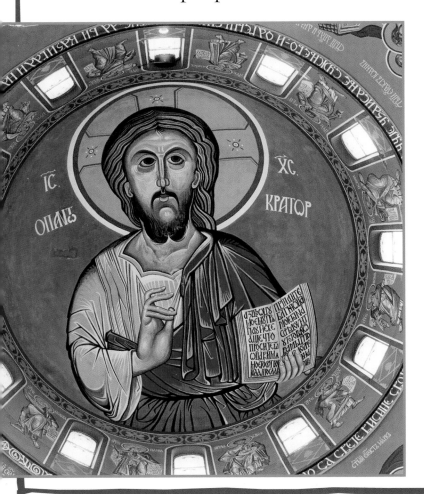

The glowing colours of these icons help people feel closer to God. For the worshippers the icons are windows into heaven.

Icon of Christ in a dome.

What else is there?

There will be some seats, often only a few around the walls. This is because people usually stand during **services**.

There is a place for the **choir**, usually near the **sanctuary**. In **Orthodox** churches the human voice is the only instrument used in **worship**, so you don't see any musical instruments. Services are sung from start to finish.

You should also be able to see a throne for the **bishop** when he visits the church. A bishop is an important church leader.

A bishop's throne.

In the sanctuary

On the **altar**, in the centre of the sanctuary, you will see the book of the **Gospels**. The Gospels are four important books in the **Bible**, the **Christian holy** book.

On a side table there is usually a special plate and cup used in **communion**. Beside them is the **incense** burner and the **banners** used in **processions**.

All of these things are richly decorated. The best things people can afford are used in worshipping **God**.

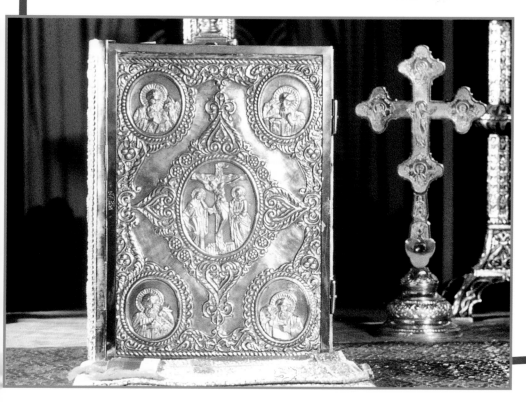

The book of the Gospels on the altar.

Who will I meet?

If you visit a church on a weekday you may see those who take care of the building and the **priest** who is in charge of the **worship**.

In the evenings and at weekends you may also meet the **deacon**, who helps the priest, and singers who come to train the **choir**. Teachers and youth club leaders come to work with groups in the **community centre** next to the church.

Lessons in the community centre.

Name days

If it is somebody's **name day** the priest may meet
a family in church. On name days he **blesses** the
special bread which they bring to church. He may
join them at home in a celebration meal.

The priest
blesses a name
day loaf.

Name days

Each **Orthodox** boy and girl has a name linked with a **saint** or a
Christian festival. As well as their birthdays, children also celebrate
the day on which their saint is remembered in the church.

Name day ceremonies are not the same in every Orthodox church.

What happens on Sundays?

Many **Christians** come to church on Sundays to celebrate **Jesus**'s **resurrection**. This is the day Christians believe **God** brought Jesus to life again, after his death on the **cross**.

This important service is called the **liturgy**. It begins at about ten or eleven o'clock and lasts up to three hours. During the liturgy **worshippers** usually stand facing the **iconostasis**. Sometimes men stand on the right and women on the left.

Worshippers facing the iconostasis.

The liturgy

During the liturgy the **priest** is helped by two or more **altar boys**. All are dressed in special robes. These show that they are leading worshippers into God's presence.

The book of the **Gospels** is carried from the **sanctuary** with lights and **incense**. This shows that Jesus's life and teaching are like a light to the world.

The priest reads part of the Gospels and explains the meaning of the reading.

The priest reading part of the Gospels with altar boys beside him.

Holy Communion

Later in the **liturgy** the **priest** carries a plate and cup in **procession** round the church. These hold bread and wine and are covered with special cloths.

The bread and wine remind **worshippers** of Jesus's last meal with his **disciples** and his death on the **cross**. The disciples were Jesus's closest followers.

Everyone bows their head as the bread and wine are carried round the church.

16

Tasting

The plate and cup are placed on the **altar**. The priest prays that **God** will use this bread and wine to enter the lives of those who take **communion**.

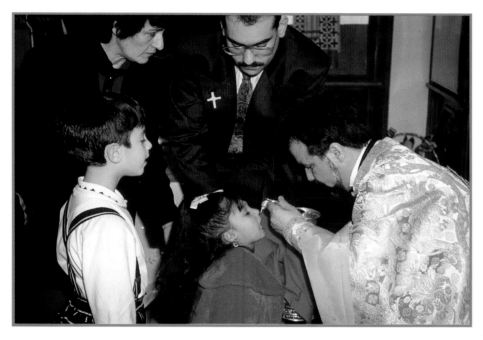

The priest uses a spoon to give communion.

While people are taking communion, the **choir** sings **hymns** and **anthems**. At the end of the liturgy everyone is invited to eat a small piece of bread. It comes from the same loaf as the bread given in communion. This shows that they all belong to the worshipping **community**.

Lent and Easter

Orthodox Christian festivals are celebrated in church. The most important is **Easter**. During Lent, the time before Easter, **worshippers fast**. People choose only a few things to eat and drink. This helps them think more about **God** and less about food.

During the week before Easter Sunday, Christians remember what happened in the last week of **Jesus**'s life. On the Friday evening, the time when Jesus was buried, an **icon** of his body is placed in a carved wooden frame which represents his **tomb**.

Girls decorating the wooden frame.

Easter Sunday

At midnight on Easter Saturday a joyful celebration of Jesus's **resurrection** begins. Some worshippers light their candle from the **priest**'s candle. Then they pass the light to others. Soon the dark church is lit by a blaze of lights. Worshippers greet each other by saying 'Christ is risen', and answering 'He is risen indeed'.

Just after midnight on Easter Sunday morning.

Festivals and ceremonies

Each year twelve other great festivals are celebrated in church. They recall events in the life of **Jesus** and Mary, his mother.

Orthodox worshippers believe their lives are gifts from **God**. From their birth they are on a journey back to God. Each important stage on the way is marked by prayers and worship.

Babies are brought to church to be baptized and **anointed** with oil. **Baptism** is the ceremony that makes babies part of the **Church**.

Preparing a baby for baptism.

More steps along life's way

Young people and adults come to tell God they are sorry for wrong things they have done.

At a wedding the **priest** crowns both bride and groom to show they are to be like a king and queen in their own family.

At someone's funeral worshippers ask God to forgive anything that person did wrong in his or her life.

The most important thing that happens in the church is linking the worshippers with God through prayer.

A bride and groom are crowned at their wedding.

Glossary

altar table in the sanctuary used during important parts of the liturgy

altar boy boy or young man who helps the priest during the liturgy

anoint touching the head and other parts of the body with a special oil

anthem song of worship sung by the choir

banner embroidered cloth, hung on a pole and carried in processions

baptism (BAP-tiz-um) ceremony making people part of the Church

Bible (BY-bull) Christian holy book

bishop Church leader in charge of all the churches in a part of a country

bless to pray that God will use people or things to bring joy and happiness

choir (KWIRE) group of singers

Christ name given to Jesus by Christians who believe he is the son of God

Christian (KRIS-tee-AN) someone who follows the religion of Christianity. Christians believe in God, and his son Jesus.

Christmas festival when Christians celebrate Jesus's birth

Church when church has a capital C, it refers to the whole Christian community

communion (kom-YOO-nee-un) eating bread and drinking wine offered to God in the liturgy

community (KOM-yoo-nittee) group of people who share the same beliefs

community centre place where a community meets

cross sign which reminds Christians of Jesus's death on the cross (usually an empty cross to show their belief in Jesus's resurrection)

deacon (dee-kun) man who helps the priest and sings a part of the liturgy

disciple one of Jesus's closest followers

dome special round roof

Easter Christian festival recalling Jesus's death and his resurrection

fasting not eating or drinking certain foods for a time, as a devotion to God

God Christians believe that God made, sees and knows everything

Gospels title of four books in the Bible, 'good news' about Jesus's life and teaching

heaven for Christians, God's home

holy means specially respected because it has to do with God

hymn song sung in church to worship God

icon (EYE-kon) holy picture painted to help people think about God

iconostasis (eye-kono-STA-sis) icon-covered screen which divides the sanctuary from the rest of the church

incense sweet smell made by burning spices

liturgy service of worship which ends with Holy Communion

Jesus Christians believe that Jesus is the son of God

name day day when the saint whose name you were given is remembered

Orthodox Greek word meaning 'right belief' and also 'right worship'. Orthodox Christianity is a kind of Christianity.

Orthodox Church when church begins with a capital C it means the whole Orthodox Christian community

priest man who performs the most important parts of the worship and cares for the lives of worshippers

procession people walking in an orderly line

resurrection (rez-erek-shun) Christian belief that God made Jesus alive again after his burial

saint person who once lived close to God and who is honoured by the Church

sanctuary part of church containing altar and other things used in worship

service meeting in church to worship God

sign of the cross gesture with the right hand, touching forehead, chest and both shoulders, reminding worshippers of Jesus's death on the cross

tomb (TOOM) hollow space cut out of rock to contain a dead body

worship (WUR-ship) show respect and love for God

worshippers people who show respect and love for God

Index